Bears, Bears, and
More Bears

Jackie Morris

Piccadilly Press • London

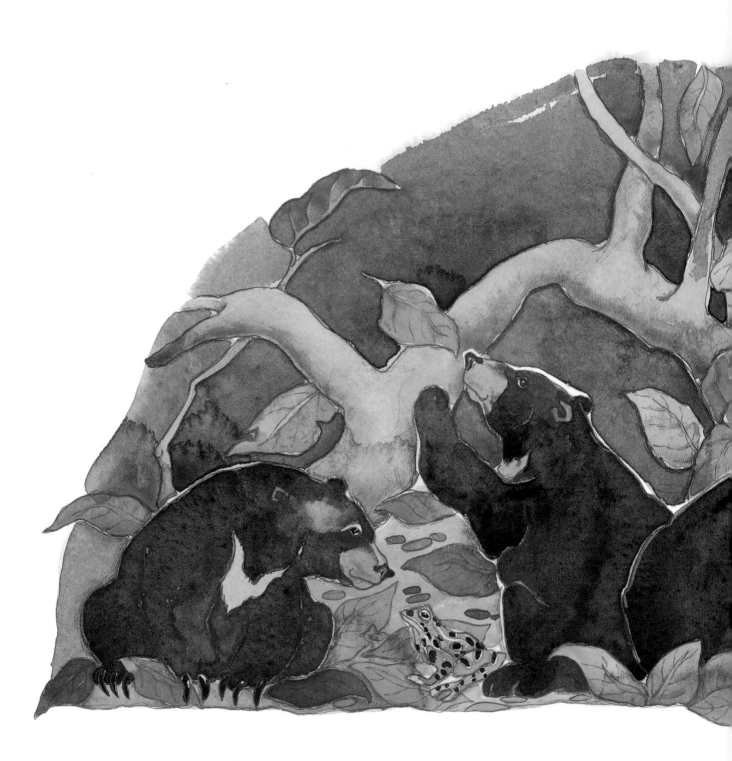

There are little bears.

There are big bears.

Bears can be black.

Bears can be brown.

Most bears sleep all winter.

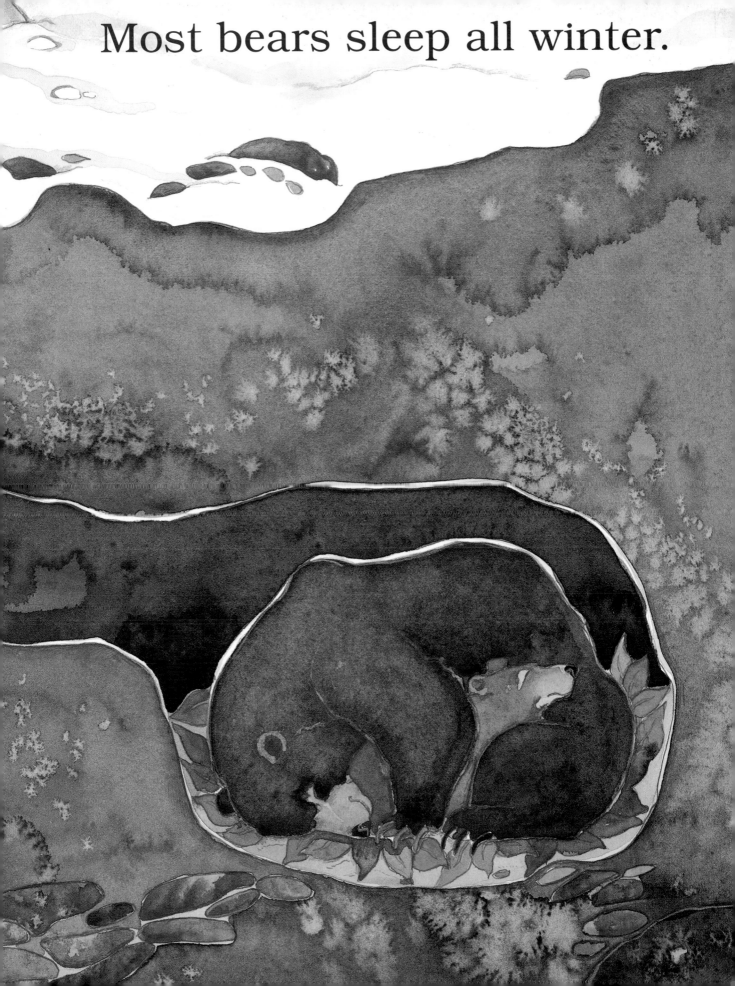

Most bears climb trees...

...run very fast,

and swim.

Some bears eat berries,

some eat fish.

Some bears eat bamboo.

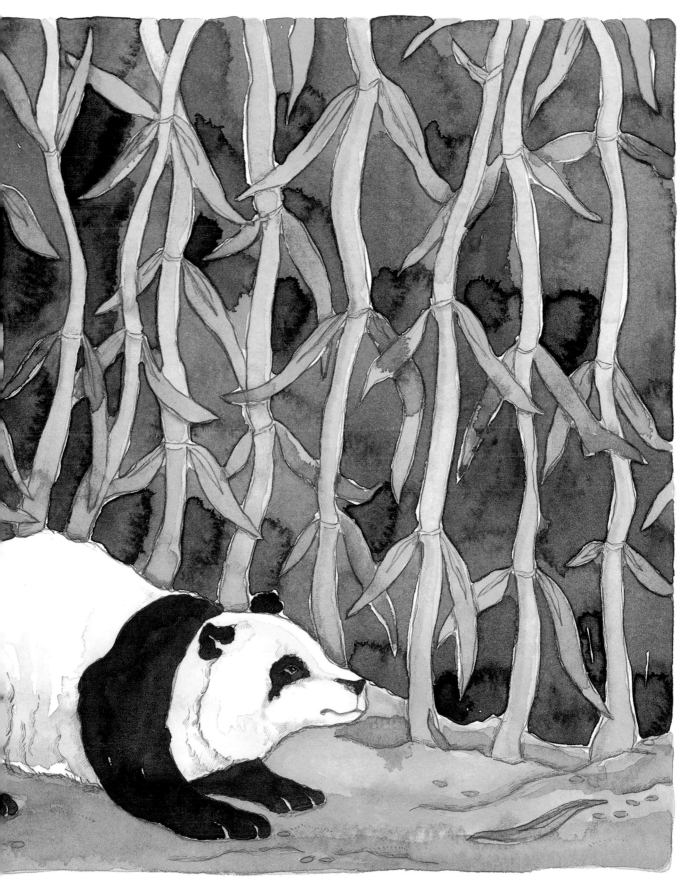

Some bears aren't

real bears at all.

are lots of bears in the world.

But the best bear is your bear.

There are little bears.

- *Sun Bears are the smallest bears.*
- *They weigh between 27 and 65 kg (60 to 145 lbs), and are 1.2 to 1.5 metres high/long (4 to 5 feet).*
- *Sun Bears are very rare.*
- *They live in the forests of South East Asia, where they are often kept as pets.*

There are big bears.

- *American Brown Bears, also called Grizzly Bears, are very big.*
- *They can weigh as much as 390 kg (800 lbs).*
- *However, the largest bear of all is the Polar Bear. It can weigh up to 600 kg (1,320 lbs) and is 2.4 to 2.6 metres (8 to 9 feet) tall/long.*

Bears can be black.

- *The Asiatic Black Bear lives in the forests and mountains of Asia.*
- *These bears have a golden crest on their chest and a mane of long black hair.*
- *There is also an American Black Bear, a large black bear with a brown muzzle.*

Bears can be brown.

- *The Brown Bear is the most common bear.*
- *Brown Bears live in Northern Canada and all over Russia.*
- *They have a distinct hump on their shoulders and very long claws on their front paws.*

Bears can even be white.

- *Polar Bears live in the Arctic where their white colour camouflages them against the snow.*
- *Their diet consists of fish, seal and the occasional walrus.*

Most bears sleep all winter.

- *Most bears sleep for between five and seven months in a year.*
- *Bears sleep in dens where the cubs are born in late winter.*
- *The dens help to keep the cubs safe when young.*
- *Bears usually have between one and four cubs, though two is the most common.*

Most bears climb trees...

- *Even the Grizzly Bear can climb trees.*
- *Bears climb mainly for safety, but they also climb to look for food, or simply to sun themselves and rest.*

...run very fast and swim.

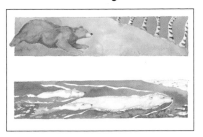

- *Bears can only run in short bursts, but they can reach high speeds.*
- *Polar Bears can run as fast as 40km (25 miles) per hour.*
- *Most bears can swim but Polar Bears swim underwater, to catch their food.*

Some bears eat berries, some eat fish.

- *Berries and roots make up 60 to 90 per cent of most bears' diet.*
- *Polar Bears usually eat fish but even they eat grass in the summer.*
- *All bears love honey.*

Some bears eat bamboo.

- *Bamboo makes up almost all of a Giant Panda's diet.*
- *Adults eat about 12.15 kg a day, sometimes eating for up to 17 hours. The rest of the time they sleep.*

Some bears aren't real bears at all.

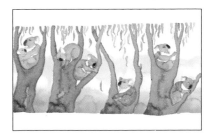

- *Koala Bears are actually marsupials, which means they carry their young in a pouch.*
- *They live in Australia and eat Eucalyptus leaves.*

To: Thomas, Charlie, Erin, William and Silas

Text and illustration copyright © Jackie Morris, 1995

Typeset and designed by Dalia Hartman
Printed by Midas, Hong Kong
for the publishers, Piccadilly Press Ltd.,
5 Castle Road, London NW1 8PR

A catalogue record for this book is available from the British Library

ISBN: 1 85340 219 2 Hardback
     1 85340 315 6 Paperback

Reprinted 2000